Advance Praise for *Leading*

Leading From Anywhere is the handbook [...] been waiting for. Tracie James combines [...] remote leadership experience with practical strategies you can use immediately to build trust, clarity, and results—no matter where your team works. Once again, Tracie has crafted an excuse-proof playbook for thriving in the new world of work.

Jonathan Sprinkles, Founder
The Connection Lab

Tracie James just handed today's leaders the playbook we've been begging for. *Leading from Anywhere* isn't fluff. It's not another "feel-good" leadership book packed with theory and buzzwords. This is a no-nonsense, practical, actionable guide that meets remote and hybrid leaders exactly where we are … stretched thin, managing teams across time zones, and craving clarity in a sea of Zoom fatigue.

Whether you're managing from a home office, a coworking space, or the airport terminal, Leading from Anywhere proves that geography doesn't define your leadership. Your systems, your clarity, and your mindset do.

If you lead people in any capacity and want to stop guessing your way through the remote revolution, get this book. Tracie James doesn't just empower you to lead from anywhere; she empowers you to lead better. Period.

Bridgett McGowen-Hawkins
Award-winning speaker, publisher, and champion of bold, brilliant leadership

Tracie has provided us with a long overdue guide to help leaders pivot in their leadership style since the pandemic. She's established a blueprint for team leaders to follow and she's taken out a lot of the "guesswork." I highly recommend this book for new, emerging, and seasoned leaders who are looking for new ways to level up their skills.

Warren Winston, AMFB
Chief Global Strategist, International Keynote Speaker, &
Global Philanthropist

This book is on the right track. As I read it, I felt like Tracie was on the sidelines watching my team and some of the struggles that we're having. Prior to the pandemic, my team was really cohesive. At the time, I didn't realize how much my hands on leadership style depended upon those in-person interactions to drive success. Being remote has been a struggle coupled with massive turnover, I've been at a lost for what to do. After reading *Leading from Anywhere*, I now have strategies I can implement with my team to gain clarity, build trust, and achieve our goals consistently.

Emanuel W. Reeves
Sr. Pharmacy Manager

As a communications, marketing, and public relations professional for nearly 11 years, I've read a few leadership books—but this one is different. It resonates with me and where I am professionally.

The principles on trust, transparency, cohesion, and prioritizing impact over busyness are already reshaping my management style (cause baby... it's been rough for the past 6 to 7 months).

I'm not only applying these strategies, but also showing my team how to use them and why they work—by example. Sharing the "why" behind decisions and fostering psychological safety has already improved our collaboration and focus on meaningful results.

This really is practical leadership in action. I will keep reading and highlighting the strategies that connect with me and help me to be a better leader.

L. Sherie Dean
Director of Marketing & Communications

Leading from Anywhere:

The No Excuses Guide to Effective Team Leadership

Tracie L. James

Leading from Anywhere:

The No Excuses Guide to Effective Team Leadership

By Tracie L. James

T. LaMorne James Enterprises, LLC
2025

DISCLAIMER
The purpose of this book is to educate and entertain. The author and publisher shall have neither liability nor responsibility for anyone with respect to any loss or damage caused, directly or indirectly, by the information contained in this book.

We don't believe in get-rich-quick programs. Your success is predicated upon your work ethic, delivering extraordinary value, and serving others with excellence.

We cannot and do not make results guarantees or give professional or legal advice.

ISBN 978-0-9990290-1-5

T. LaMorne James Enterprises, LLC
14053 Memorial Drive #435, Houston, TX 77079
www.tracieljames.com

*My **FREE gift** to you for buying this book, you have access to special tools and resources to help you lead anywhere. Visit TracieLJames.com/remoteleader to download.*

Dedication

This book is dedicated to the amazing leaders I've worked alongside who showed me what was possible through their courage, compassion, conviction, and often their quiet strength. Thank you for modeling what it means to lead with integrity, to lift others while rising, and to never lose sight of the person behind the results. Your example guided me along my leadership journey and this book is my way of sharing what I've learned along the way from each of you.

Acknowledgments

Writing this book has been a journey filled with reflection, growth, and immense gratitude. I am deeply thankful to the leaders who have shaped my understanding of what it truly means to be a great leader. Your impact goes far beyond titles, sales, or customers. You taught me that leadership is about people, purpose, and impact. Special shout out to Norman, Stephanie, Lauri, Byron, Greg, Lynette, Amanda, Jenny, and Felicia!! You've been a light in my career!!

To my mentors, accountability partners and my front row, thank you for your wisdom, your honesty, and the push to keep growing even when it was uncomfortable. You challenged me to be authentic and lead from my heart. Thank you Bridgett, Alexis, Shana, Monique, Michelle, and Christy... you never let me give up!!

To my colleagues and clients, thank you for trusting me with your teams, your goals, and your challenges. Your stories and experiences are woven into the fabric of this book. My goal is to keep getting better so I can continue to help you grow your businesses.

To my family, your unwavering support gave me the courage and space to write. Thank you for believing in this vision from day one and for being patient when I wasn't as available.

And to every reader holding this book: I wrote this for you. May it encourage you, challenge you, and remind you of the powerful influence you hold as a leader. I challenge you to lead authentically... NO EXCUSES!

Table of Contents

Introduction

Introduction

The New Frontier of Leadership

"You do not rise to the level of your goals. You fall to the level of your systems." James Clear

In the not-so-distant past, leadership was defined by proximity. Leaders walked the floor, read body language in meetings, and used in-person visibility as a measure of productivity. But the world of work has changed and it's not going back despite how hard many companies are pushing for a full return to the office.

This seismic shift to hybrid and remote operations is new to so many companies and industries. Remote teams, once an occasional experiment or a perk, are now a cornerstone of how organizations operate. This transformation has redefined what it means to lead, presenting both unprecedented opportunities and unique challenges. The question is: How do you ensure your team that's spread across cities, time zones, and even continents not only perform but thrives?

Whether you lead a hybrid team, manage contractors across time zones, or run a business from your kitchen table, the truth is this: you're already leading from anywhere. The question is "Are you doing it well?"

My Journey to Leading Anywhere

I've worked remotely most of my over 30-year career. I was hired for my first outside sales position in 1996, just 2 years after I completed my undergrad degree. Since then, my boss has been in another state more often than not. I enjoyed this because it gave me flexibility and autonomy on how I managed my work.

Contrary to popular belief, I wasn't working from my bed or not doing my work. On the other hand, I was more engaged because I knew my success was connected to my sales success which required focused effort working with my clients.

When I first transitioned to managing others remotely, I struggled. I was so used to the in-person management dynamics of office life: impromptu hallway conversations, immediate feedback, and the ability to gauge team morale with a glance. Remote work stripped away those comforts, and I found myself overcompensating with endless check-ins and overly detailed instructions. My team felt suffocated, and I felt exhausted. My boss helped me understand that I needed to manage my team the same way he managed me when I was in their position.

This conversation shifted my approach, and I began to trust my team, set clear expectations, and focused on outcomes rather than processes that everything changed. Productivity soared, engagement improved, and I discovered a more sustainable way to lead. This book is the culmination of those lessons and the strategies I've developed over years of leading high-performing teams remotely.

What to Expect in This Book

This book is your no-excuses guide to becoming an effective, outcomes-driven team leader in a remote world. There is an art to leading remote teams. It's not about theory or fluffy inspiration. It's about clarity, systems, and action. It's about creating an environment where excuses have no room to grow. It's about building a culture of accountability, trust, and excellence, no matter where your team members are located.

It is divided into actionable, easy-to-follow chapters that address the most pressing challenges of remote leadership.

Lead Anywhere
No Excuses Strategy

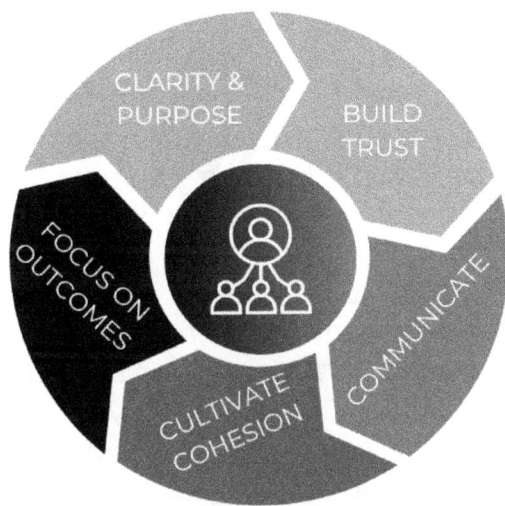

CLARITY & PURPOSE

BUILD TRUST

FOCUS ON OUTCOMES

COMMUNICATE

CULTIVATE COHESION

You'll learn how to:
- Align your team around purpose, priorities, and performance
- Build trust across distance and difference
- Communicate with intention (and fewer meetings)
- Create cohesion without relying on the office
- Focus on results instead of busyness
- Develop your own repeatable leadership playbook

Each chapter is designed to be practical and immediately applicable. You'll find real-world examples, common leadership pitfalls, and a clear framework to help you lead with confidence no matter where you or your team are located. This isn't just a book to read. It's a toolkit to implement.

How to Use This Book

You can approach this book in several ways:

- Read it cover-to-cover for a comprehensive playbook to excuse-proof leadership.
- Focus on specific chapters that address your immediate challenges.
- Use the actionable takeaways to test strategies with your team and refine your approach.

Leadership is not one-size-fits-all, and neither is this book. Adapt the insights to suit your unique style and team dynamics. Leadership is a journey, and this book is designed to meet you wherever you are.

Who This Book Is For

Are you a leader managing a remote or hybrid team? Are you an aspiring manager eager to build strong leadership foundations? Or perhaps you're an HR professional or business owner looking for practical tools to empower your workforce. No matter your title, if you're navigating the complexities of remote leadership, this book is for you.

The principles of leading anywhere apply across industries, team sizes, and location. Whether you're leading a small startup or overseeing a global organization, the strategies in this book will help you unlock your team's potential and drive exceptional results.

Why This Book Now?

Because "remote" isn't the exception anymore. It's become the norm. Leaders can't rely on charisma or chaos. They need systems that support clarity, accountability, and autonomy. Recent reports show that over 92% of professionals now work remotely at least one day a week, and many companies have embraced hybrid or fully remote models.[1] This shift has brought undeniable benefits, like increased productivity, access to a global talent pool, and improved work-life balance.

Remote work has been associated with increased productivity in various sectors. A study by the U.S. Bureau of Labor Statistics found that total factor productivity growth from 2019 to 2021 was positively associated with the rise in remote work across 61 industries in the private business sector.[2]

In a world where uncertainty is the norm, your ability to lead with consistency is your competitive edge. Leadership is no longer about being in the room. It's about how you show up everywhere.

A Call to Action
Leading a remote team is not without its challenges, but it's also an opportunity to build something extraordinary. By embracing excuse-proof leadership, you can create a culture where accountability, trust, and innovation thrive. This journey requires effort, but the rewards of a high-performing, engaged, and resilient team are so worth it.

Welcome to the new frontier of leadership. Your team's success starts with you. Let's get to work.

Excuse-Proof Reflection
Journal your responses:

1. What issues currently exist within your remote/hybrid team?

   _____

   _____

   _____

   _____

2. How are you currently addressing these issues?

   _____

   _____

   _____

   _____

3. After what you've discovered so far, are you starting to see opportunities to address these issues in a new way? Are you wondering what's possible if you keep going?

   _____

   _____

   _____

   _____

Chapter 1

Chapter 1

Lead with Clarity and Purpose

"If you don't know where you're going, you'll end up someplace else." Yogi Berra

Leading with clarity means communicating a focused vision, shared values, and defined expectations. When team members know exactly where they're headed, what matters, and how their work contributes, they move forward with purpose and confidence even when working miles apart.

Leadership Reality Check

While working for Sara Lee HBC, I worked remotely with brokers who assisted with the distribution of our skincare line to independent beauty suppliers across the United States. My brokers covered a specific region, so I worked with each one independently. At first, I was overwhelmed. My new position came with more responsibility, higher financial goals, and more travel. I went from traveling only in my car to flying all over the country.

I learned the lesson on the importance of leading with clarity during the first quarter. I was pumped and ready to be successful. I was the youngest person in my position for any brand in the division, so I knew I had to prove myself. The first quarter did not go well. I struggled to get a handle on my accounts. I managed both national retailers and brokers who worked with the independents. When I reviewed my numbers, I was not happy with my performance at all. I missed every target.

I immediately set up calls with each of my brokers to discuss what had gone wrong during my transition. I immediately saw what went wrong. I had meetings with each of them during my first month and we discussed goals, but I realized that they weren't clear on the goal, how we could get there and what it really meant for them. This was my "aha" moment.

In a remote world, clarity isn't optional... it's REQUIRED of every leader. When teams aren't physically together, even small miscommunications can become major productivity blockers. In the absence of real-time feedback loops, assumptions grow, confidence shrinks, and alignment weakens. If team members aren't clear on the mission, their role, or the destination, they won't perform well. They will get off task, miss the goal and the team will suffer.

Leaders often miss out on opportunities for success because their vision was unclear, or the vision was not effectively conveyed to their team. Your vision must be clearly defined. Lewis Carroll says, "Any road will get you there, if you don't know where you are going." Knowing you want to be successful is not enough to make your vision a reality. Great leaders are focused and driven. You must clearly define everything in writing. This will provide the clarity and purpose for your team.

Principle in Focus
As a leader, when you make the vision clear and outline a clear path to that vision, you're setting the stage for your team's success. The structure and organization are needed to keep everyone on the same page. The written document is there for reference as a reminder to everyone on the team.

The best remote leaders don't just delegate tasks. They provide the direction, define the purpose, and remove any ambiguity. Clarity is more than communication. It's strategic and intentional in how it creates alignment for your team's work. When people know what's expected and why it matters, they take ownership and move with more confidence.

Leading with clarity and purpose is effective not only professionally, but also personally. You can begin to truly live your life when you have clearly defined your vision, goals, and purpose. Otherwise, life is living you. Help yourself and your team by putting in the work on the front end so that your success will be on the back end.

Why It Matters
Studies from Gallup and Harvard Business Review show that employees who strongly agree they know what's expected of them are over 20% more productive and engaged.[3] In remote environments, lack of clarity causes decision delays, rework, and disengagement. Teams don't need more meetings. They need more meaning.

There have been numerous articles written over the years about the importance of writing down our goals, but so many still just think about their goals. When you write down your goals and regularly focus on them, you're 42% more likely to achieve them based on a study conducted by Dr. Gail Matthews at Dominican University in California.[4] Writing down your goals connects the right and left hemispheres of the brain by taking what you see in your imagination and writing it down to connect with the logical side. Creating that connection increases your ability to make the needed changes to accomplish your goals.

Written goals will help your team take ownership of the goals that are set. Researchers at Cornell University found that the "endowment effect" occurs when a person takes ownership of something.[5] Giving your team clear goals that they can own from beginning to end with increase their dedication, commitment, and ultimate success.

In an office, ambiguity might be smoothed over by proximity. You can tap someone on the shoulder, overhear a conversation, or course-correct quickly. But in a distributed environment, ambiguity becomes a silent productivity killer.

Remote leaders can't afford to be vague. Clarity is not a "nice to have"... it's a strategic imperative.

Clarity answers questions like:
- What are we working toward?
- What does success look like?
- Who owns what?
- What matters most right now?

Without these answers, teams drift. With them, they move with purpose.

Common Pitfalls
In leadership, it's your job to identify potential pitfalls and establish a plan for overcoming them. As you work with your team, you will begin to assess the pitfalls. Don't allow them to lead to excuses. Let's eliminate these excuses on the front end by asking questions and putting contingencies in place for them. Here are a few common pitfalls when it comes to clarity and purpose.

- Vague Goals: "Do your best" isn't direction. It's ambiguity.

- Misaligned Priorities: When everything feels urgent, nothing is truly prioritized.
- Unclear Roles: Confusion over responsibilities leads to duplicated or dropped work.
- Assumed Understanding: Leaders assume people "get it" without confirming.

So how do you do lead with clarity and purpose, especially in a remote environment?

To eliminate ambiguity, use the **No Excuses Clarity Strategy:**

No Excuses
Clarity Strategy

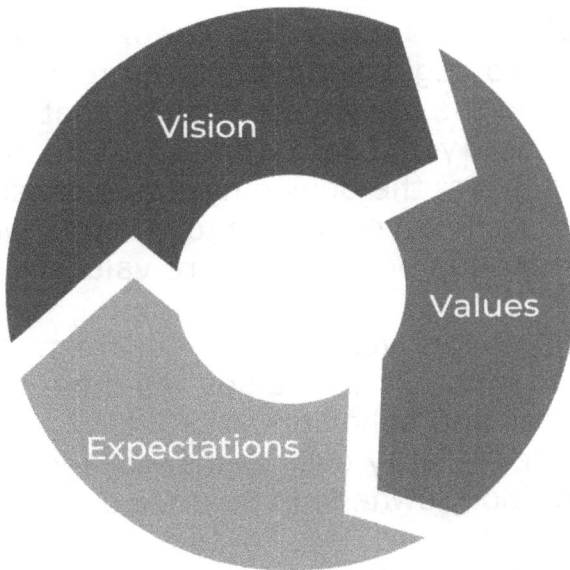

Vision

Values

Expectations

Step 1: Vision → Define the Destination

You start by painting the bigger picture for your team. Don't just say it once. You must repeatedly articulate the why behind the work. Connect your team's daily tasks and goals to this purpose so they will feel connected to the company's mission. A to do list is not motivating or inspirational. In sales, it was easy to see the connection with what we did each day. For those outside of sales, they needed to be shown how their work supported the company's success.

- Craft a one-sentence statement that captures the team's focus.
- Template: "Our purpose this quarter is to [achieve X] so that [desired impact]."
- Example: "Our purpose this quarter is to streamline onboarding so new hires can contribute within 14 days."

Step 2: Values → Anchor the Team Culture

You will need to begin cultivating your team's culture by clearly defining the team's core values that will provide direction for how your team works. Talking about culture once is just the beginning. It's a constant process that's refined over time to create a workplace that's grounded in your team's core values.

- Identify 3 core values with your team. Allow them to have input. These values will drive daily decisions and behaviors.
- Example: "Clarity over chaos, collaboration over competition, ownership over excuses."

We will discuss cultivating team cohesion and culture in Chapter 4.

Step 3: Expectations → Set Clear Roles & Results

Define the roles and set clear, measurable goals for each team member. Make sure their goals connect to the company's overall goals. If there's a disconnect, they will be working toward something that's out of line with the overall vision. These priorities should be shared with the entire team and success should be clearly defined. Transparency is key. In sales, we received weekly reports on our numbers so there were no surprises at the end of the month, quarter, or year. We knew exactly where we stood. Every team member should know what Key Performance Indicators (KPIs) they are expected to meet. Take the time to do this and you will be amazed at how it leads to success.

- Outline who owns what, and what success looks like for each team member and the team as a whole.
- Use 1x1s to align on top 3 priorities
- Ask, "How will we know this week was a win?"

Individual accountability drives clarity and purpose forward. Once expectations are clearly defined, it's up to each team member to own their role, follow through on commitments, and align their actions with the team's vision. Without accountability, even the clearest goals become meaningless. Leaders who foster a culture of ownership empower their teams to move with focus, integrity, and intentionality.

Quick Wins

Looking for a quick win this week, implement the following:

- Rewrite your team vision in one clear sentence.
- Create a one-pager that outlines team priorities and key outcomes.
- Schedule alignment 1X1s with each team member to review roles.

Leadership in Action

After I clarified the goals and the path to them by writing everything down and ensuring they understood the purpose of what we were working to achieve. Honestly, they needed to know how they would benefit from working with me. Leading with clarity would ensure success for everyone.

Going forward, I sent them the goals for the quarter, and we met weekly discuss our progress and identify any issues. I asked for their suggestions and feedback on what was happening in their market. I scheduled time to work alongside them in their markets so I could gain a better understanding of their accounts and any challenges they were facing. By the end of the next quarter, I was seeing improvements. The last two quarters of the year got me back on track to not only meet the year end goal, but to exceed it by 15%. We added new accounts and increased sales within existing accounts.

Overall, I gained the support of each broker because I invested the time in them and their businesses. I had to do more than throw a number at them. I had to help them plan and assess consistently. Since my brand was one of many brands they represented, I had to provide them with quality information consistently to remain top of mind. We became a team because they knew I wanted them to meet their personal goals as well. We worked together to make sure we both succeeded.

Real World Example

GitLab is an excellent example of leading with clarity and purpose. GitLab is a pioneer in all-remote work, with over 1,500 employees in 60+ countries. They've built their operations around one principle: clarity enables autonomy.

Their entire team handbook is publicly accessible. This handbook outlines everything from communication protocols to performance reviews. All decisions are documented. Every role is explicitly defined. Expectations are visible to everyone. I absolutely love this!! This handbook leaves no room for confusion.

The company can operate seamlessly across time zones and avoid bottlenecks. Their culture is dictated in this handbook, and it empowers employees to take initiative without waiting for instructions. "If it's not in the handbook, it doesn't exist." GitLab Leadership Principle[6]

I love the foresight of the founders. They began this handbook when they only had ten employees. They found this format to be efficient and easy to share information with everyone. It enables new employees to see how the company operates from day one. It outlines who they are and how they communicate. Since the handbook is extensive and updated regularly, it remains relevant as the company grows and evolves.

The company cites the following benefits[7]:
- Reading is much faster than listening.
- Reading is async, you don't have to interrupt someone or wait for them to become available.
- Talent Acquisition is easier if people can see what we stand for and how we operate.
- Retention is better if people know what they are getting into before they join.
- On-boarding is easier if you can find all relevant information spelled out.
- Teamwork is easier if you can read how other parts of the company work.
- Discussing changes is easier if you can read what the current process is.
- Communicating change is easier if you can just point to the diff.

- Everyone can contribute to it by proposing a change via a merge request.

One cool thing about this handbook is they say it's "far from rigid… GitLab will review each team member's concern or situation based on local laws to determine the best outcome and then update the handbook accordingly."

In summary, to lead with clarity and purpose, you must first clearly share the vision, goals, and the plan for achieving them with your team. Each person must understand how what they do each day helps the company be successful. This is not a one and done conversation. You must reflect on the vision regularly to ensure it becomes second nature. You want your team to make decisions, solve problems and be innovative with the vision in mind.

In the next chapter, we will discuss the importance of building trust with your team and how to effectively establish this trust regardless of where you and your team work each day.

Excuse-Proof Reflection

Journal your responses:

1. Where are you assuming clarity exists but haven't confirmed it?

   _____

   _____

   _____

   _____

2. How well does my team understand the why behind our work?

   _____

   _____

   _____

   _____

3. Do my team members know what "a win" looks like each week? If yes, describe it here.

   _____

   _____

   _____

   _____

4. Think of a recent project or task where your team seemed confused, misaligned, or hesitant. What assumptions did you make about what was "clear"? How could you reframe or re-communicate that task with better purpose and expectations?

   _____

   _____

   _____

   _____

Resource Download

Grab the free Leadership Clarity Audit and Leadership One-Pager at TracieLJames.com/remoteleader. Use them to apply this chapter's strategy right away.

Chapter 2

Chapter 2

Build and Maintain Trust

"Trust is built in very small moments." Brené Brown

Now that you've created clarity and purpose with your team, you have a good foundation to build trust. Most importantly, you must understand that trust doesn't grow on its own. It must be cultivated as a part of your leadership. Trust is the currency of leadership. Without it, even the best strategies fall flat.

Leadership Reality Check
I led a high-performing event team, but after the project began, we had issues with people our regular meetings. People would arrive late, leave early or not show up at all. In addition, key tasks were going undone. Without their full commitment, the overall project was in danger of failing. I decided to schedule individual meetings with each person to discuss the issues and to find out what was causing the disconnect. I was surprised that none of them understood why they were needed since the client had hired me. They expected me to handle everything, which normally I would, but they were involved at the insistence of the client. They thought I was expecting them to do my job, which they resented. I realized that trust isn't automatic. It has to be earned over time by what you say and do aligning consistently.

In remote teams, there's no water cooler. No body language. No instant "vibe check" after a meeting. Without intention, trust decays. And without trust, performance and culture unravel. People start to question motives, hoard information, and disengage.

Remote leaders can't afford to be passive about trust. It must be proactively built and consistently reinforced.

Without trust, employees can feel micromanaged, disconnected, and/or unmotivated. Establishing trust requires consistent effort and intentionality. Start with being upfront about expectations, goals, and challenges (Chapter 1). Transparency creates an environment where team members feel included and valued. You must show trust to earn trust. Let your employees know you have faith in their abilities by not micromanaging. It will take time to build genuine connections beyond the work.

Principle in Focus
Trust in leadership means your team believes:
- You'll do what you say
- You care about their success
- You'll create a safe environment for contribution and candor

In remote and hybrid settings, trust must be actively built. It doesn't just happen through daily interactions. Your actions must be consistent, visible, and values aligned.

In remote work, trust replaces proximity. Leaders must trust their teams to perform without constant oversight, and teams must trust their leaders to provide clear direction and support. You build trust by being transparent, consistent, and approachable. When mistakes happen, treat them as learning opportunities not failures. Be open to share your own challenges to cultivate openness and demonstrate vulnerability.

Trust is foundational to building strong, engaged, and high-performing teams. Trust fosters a positive work environment, encouraging teamwork, problem-solving, and innovation. It fosters a sense of responsibility and responsibility, reducing turnover and reducing the likelihood of seeking other opportunities. Trusting leaders also reduce turnover by holding employees accountable and viewing their work as a partnership with their leader.

Over time, teams led by effective leaders create a culture of respect, loyalty, and shared purpose. Trust enables teams to handle crises with confidence, knowing their leader will provide guidance and support. With trust as a foundation, employees feel empowered to think creatively and take calculated risks, driving long-term organizational success.

Why It Matters
Google's Project Aristotle[8] found that psychological safety, the feeling of being safe to take risk, is the #1 predictor of high-performing teams.

Teams with high trust:
- Collaborate more effectively
- Recover from mistakes faster
- Feel more committed to shared goals

In contrast, teams that lack trust default to self-preservation and siloed thinking.

Great leaders create an atmosphere where people feel safe, seen, and supported. Trust isn't earned by checking productivity. It's built through transparency, consistency, and care. In the absence of physical presence, leaders must lead with emotional presence.

Common Pitfalls
As a team leader, it's your job to build trust with your team by overcoming any pitfalls. Avoid making excuses about why building trust is difficult in a remote

environment. Focus on fixing them instead of how it's not easy to accomplish. Be intentional with your actions. Here are a few common pitfalls when it comes to building trust.

- Inconsistency: Saying one thing, doing another
- Micromanagement: Undermines confidence and signals distrust
- Poor Follow-Through: Missed deadlines, skipped 1X1s, broken promises
- Surface-Level Relationships: Lack of real connection creates distance and doubt

Key Barrier to Building Trust

In a remote environment, it can be tempting to become a micromanager, but you must trust your team to do their job. Don't create additional work for your team and yourself because you can't let go of control. Trust the professionals you've hired to do their jobs.

Delegation is not always an easy task to accomplish and requires you to be confident in yourself and your abilities, while trusting others and their abilities. Consider delegation to be an opportunity to develop your team and reduce your own stress. Once you've established clarity and purpose, you and your team are on the same page. Trust them to do their part and they will trust you to do yours. When you commit to trusting your team, they will step up and perform at a high-level.

No-Excuses Trust Building Strategy

Trust is built through three repeatable behaviors regardless of where you lead:

No Excuses
Trust Building
Strategy

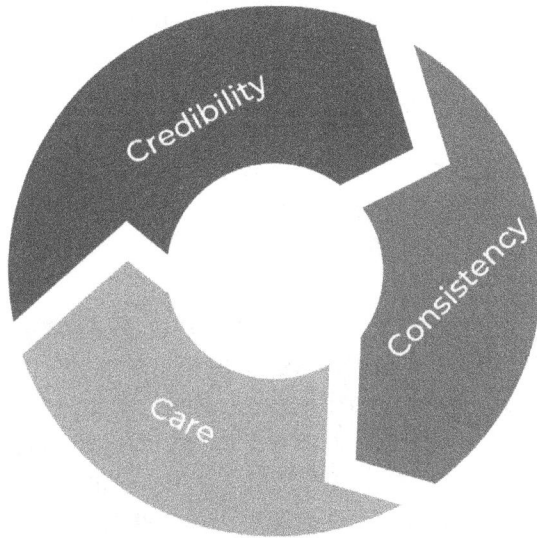

Step 1: Credibility → Know Your Stuff and Deliver
Be willing to share the why behind decisions. Give your team an understanding of why things are being done. Be honest about any challenges or issues the company is currently facing. As a leader, I know there are times where you know things you've been instructed not to share. My team always appreciated my willingness to be honest and say that I will share once I've been cleared to share. This openness helps to reduce ambiguity and anxiety. They will be confident in you and your leadership ability. It's your job to provide context, especially for your remote team.

- Be transparent about what you know and don't know
- Admit mistakes and fix them quickly
- Be open to reduce ambiguity and anxiety

Step 2: Consistency → Show Up Consistently

Be consistent in when and how you communicate. Make yourself available to your team consistently. Prioritize your time with your team. Trust builds when your team knows what to expect from you. Be a leader that keeps their word and effectively communicates when it's not possible.

- Be reliable in words and actions
- Hold regular 1x1s and team check-ins
- Stick to team agreements (e.g., response times, deadlines)

Step 3: Care → Be Human, Not a Manager

Allow yourself to be seen as human by your team. Let them know you make mistakes and that you're someone who believes that failure is a learning opportunity. Model authenticity and encourage them to do the same. This will help them feel more comfortable sharing with you without fear of retribution. Provide opportunities for them to share their ideas for change and innovation. Show your team you care about them by asking about their lives outside work. Remember you lead people and manage things.

- Ask about goals beyond the task list
- Acknowledge effort, not just results
- Make space for honest conversations and feedback

Be mindful that toxic workplace trauma, like being micromanaged, being left out, or broken promises, can make it hard for a team to build trust. These experiences leave emotional scars that make team members hesitant to give feedback or doubt other's intentions. As a remote leader, it's important to be aware of these hidden wounds and work to rebuild trust

———

through consistency, openness, and understanding. Without that work, trauma from the past can quietly ruin even the best-laid plans for psychological safety and teamwork.

Quick Wins
Looking for a quick win this week, implement the following:
- Schedule or recommit to recurring 1x1s with each team member
- Ask this question in your next meeting: "What's one thing I could do to better support you?"
- Acknowledge one person's effort publicly this week. Focus on behaviors that build trust *(ownership, vulnerability, collaboration)*

Leadership in Action
After being told they felt taken advantage of, I contacted my client and arranged a meeting. During this meeting, she explained to them why she wanted them to work with me on the project and to get their commitment to be fully engaged in the project. Her team needed to know that I wasn't using my team because she wanted hers involved in the process. They needed to understand that they were doing the part that she didn't contract my team to do.

After this meeting, things turned around. Once they understood the why and that they weren't being used, they fully engaged, and our work relationship improved. Trust was established when all the confusion and ambiguity about the project were removed. The project went smoothly, and we produced an amazing event that was profitable and an enjoyable experience for everyone in attendance.

Real World Example

Buffer, a remote-first social media company, is famous for publishing internal metrics, salaries, and even company decisions publicly. This transparency is a trust strategy. I admire their willingness to be so transparent in a world where corporations are notorious for hiding things not only from the general public but also from their employees.

They have been intentional about how their managers conduct 1x1s with their team. It's focused on the whole person, not just work-related metrics. They ask open ended questions and focus on supporting their team's mental health. Their leadership shows that they trust their employees and that trust is returned tenfold in engagement and performance. "Transparency breeds trust, and trust is the foundation of great teamwork." Joel Gascoigne, CEO of Buffer.[9]

In summary, cultivating trust enables employees to feel empowered, engaged, and loyal, which, in turn, leads to team and organizational success. A leader who prioritizes trust not only strengthens the team's performance but also builds a legacy of integrity and collaboration.

In the next chapter, we will discuss effective communication, which is a key element of building trust with your team.

Excuse-Proof Reflection

Journal your responses:

1. Do you show up in ways that make people feel safe, seen, and supported? If yes, describe how.

_____

_____

_____

_____

2. Where have you unintentionally eroded trust through inconsistency? Be detailed.

_____

_____

_____

_____

3. What's one action you can take this week to demonstrate credibility, consistency, or care?

_____

_____

_____

_____

4. Consider the last 1x1 you had with a team member. Did you focus only on tasks, or also on how they're doing as a person? What's one way you could deepen trust with your team this week through openness, consistency, or empathy?

_____

_____

_____

_____

Resource Download

Download the 1X1 Conversation Guide and the Team Trust Survey at TracieLJames.com/remoteleader. These tools will help you measure and strengthen trust starting this week.

Chapter 3

Chapter 3

Communicate Intentionally

"The single biggest problem in communication is the illusion that it has taken place." George Bernard Shaw

Clear, purposeful communication builds alignment, accountability, and connection, especially in remote and hybrid environments. In remote teams, silence isn't golden. It's confusing. Don't assume everything is good if your team isn't asking questions. It doesn't mean there are no questions in the minds of your team.

Leadership Reality Check
A few years ago, I had a client who took over as the general manager of a retail business with both in-person and remote employees. She entered the business and found so much resistance, disconnection, and lack of communication and collaboration. Everyone was so possessive of their jobs and didn't want anyone else to know what they were doing. They all had excuses for why they didn't see the need for meetings, sharing information or collaboration. I recommended that she work with everyone separately to get to the root of the issue. People tend to open up more without an audience. She was able to build trust with several key employees and she found that everyone was afraid of being replaced. The prior management pitted employees against each other to get them to work long hours and to do work that was outside of their core role. This created the disconnected, competitive environment that was destroying the business from the inside out. My client had to find a way to fix the lack of communication and collaboration to keep her job.

When communication slows down or becomes inconsistent in a remote team, people fill the gaps with assumptions and usually not the positive kind. Lack of visibility can create feelings of isolation, confusion, or even fear. On the other hand, poor-quality communication that is vague updates, excessive meetings, or unclear feedback can add friction instead of clarity.

Communicating effectively with a remote team presents a unique set of challenges that go beyond simply replacing in-person meetings with video calls. One of the most significant obstacles is the absence of nonverbal cues. In a virtual setting, leaders can't easily read facial expressions, tone of voice, or body language, which often help convey emotions, intentions, or concerns. This lack of context can lead to misunderstandings or misinterpretations, especially when messages are delivered via email or chat. Additionally, without the informal moments that happen in physical workplaces, like quick hallway conversations or spontaneous check-ins, leaders miss out on opportunities to connect personally and build rapport.

Another major challenge is maintaining clarity, consistency, and engagement across multiple communication platforms. Remote teams often rely on a mix of emails, messaging apps, video calls, and project management tools, which can lead to fragmented communication and information overload. When messages are scattered across different channels, team members may struggle to prioritize tasks or fully understand expectations. This complexity is compounded when teams operate across different time zones, making it difficult to schedule real-time conversations or maintain a shared rhythm. As a result, some employees may feel disconnected from the team's mission or excluded from key decisions.

—

Furthermore, remote work environments can make it harder to foster trust, accountability, and psychological safety. In a physical office, leaders can casually observe how their teams are doing and address issues in the moment. Remotely, those touchpoints must be intentional—and often more structured—which can feel impersonal or forced. Without clear communication and follow-up, leaders may struggle to hold team members accountable or notice early signs of disengagement. Over time, this can impact morale, collaboration, and overall team performance. Leaders must be proactive in creating space for honest dialogue, offering support, and ensuring everyone feels seen and heard despite the distance.

Principle in Focus
Remote leaders must not only communicate more often; they must communicate more intentionally. That means choosing the right channel, the right tone, and the right level of detail based on context. Overcommunication is better than under-communication, but alignment beats noise every time.

Effective communication is the cornerstone of leadership and team performance. Enhanced communication skills can improve understanding, cultivate collaboration, resolve conflicts, and build stronger relationships within the team. In a remote work environment, communication is not imperative for your team's success. Without the casual conversations and visual cues that naturally occur in an office setting, remote teams rely entirely on intentional and structured communication to function effectively. A missed email, a misinterpreted tone in a message, or unclear instructions can snowball into larger issues, derailing projects and creating frustration.

As the leader, your ability to communicate clearly and consistently can make or break your team's ability to succeed. In this chapter, we'll explore the principles, tools, and strategies that ensure your messages are heard, understood, and acted upon.

Intentional communication means choosing the right message, for the right audience, using the right method, at the right time. It's not about saying more, but it's about communicating with clarity and impact. Remote teams don't benefit from hallway chats or spontaneous alignment. Leaders must architect their communication with purpose.

Why It Matters

Effective communication is challenging even when in person. In a remote environment, these challenges are amplified. The lack of non-verbal cues i.e., body language, facial expressions, or tone can cause messages to be misinterpreted. Remote team members can work in different time zones which requires everyone to learn to navigate asynchronous communication. In addition, there is a risk of both overcommunication and under communication. Overloading team members with messages can be just as harmful as leaving them in the dark.

At the same time, clear communication offers immense benefits. It aligns your team and ensures everyone understands their roles and the goals they're working toward. It can prevent conflict by reducing misunderstandings that could lead to disputes. Transparent communication builds trust and cultivates a sense of belonging. Overall, it can improve team morale and productivity.

According to a report by McKinsey[10], teams that communicate effectively are 3.5x more likely to

outperform their peers. Intentional communication:
- Builds alignment around goals
- Reduces misunderstandings
- Creates space for healthy dialogue and feedback

Without it, teams will default to assumptions, confusion, and information overload. As a result, your team performance will suffer.

Effective communication is one of the keys to a successful team. When leaders work with their team, they are better able to establish open lines of communication – formally and informally. Alex Pentland at MIT's Human Dynamics Laboratory[11] took on the task of identifying what makes a great team.

The study found the following:
- Communicate frequently.
- Talk and listen in equal measure, equally among members.
- Engage in frequent informal communication.
- Explore for ideas and information outside the group.

The key connector in each of these areas is communication. So, it is imperative that you work with your team to build the lines of communication with everyone. The benefits will be increased interaction, conflict resolution, clear understanding of individual responsibilities, and informal training.

Common Pitfalls
It's important to address how communication can breakdown. Communication breakdowns can happen even when the best practices are followed. Take proactive measures to address them.
Determine the underlying causes and determine how you will overcome them.

- Over-communication: Excessive messages dilute importance
- Under-communication: Key updates get buried or missed
- Wrong channels: Using email for urgent issues or chat for complex topics
- Lack of clarity: Vague instructions or outcomes
- Different Audiences: Exact same messages instead of a tailored message

No-Excuses Communication Strategy

In a remote environment, communication is the bridge that connects your team's efforts. Effective communication requires clarity, consistency, and intentionality. Follow the 4Ds to improve your team's communication.

No Excuses
Communication Strategy

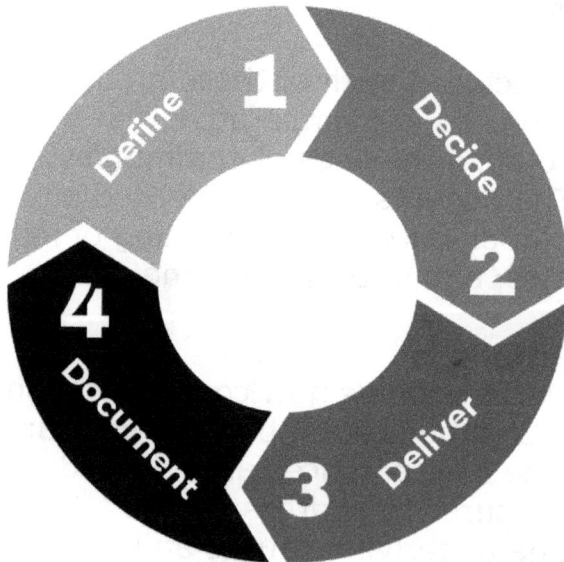

Use the 4Ds of the No Excuses Communication Strategy to communicate with impact:

Step 1: Define → What's the Message?
Use simple, straightforward language to convey your message. Avoid unclear statements that require too much follow up.
- Be clear on what you're trying to say
- Focus on the "one big thing" per message
- Example: Instead of "Let's touch base," try "We need to finalize the campaign goals by Friday."

Step 2: Decide → Who Needs to Know?
Only share information with those who need to receive it. This will reduce the overload of overcommunicating. Not every message should be sent to everyone on the team.
- Tailor the message for relevance and/or audience
- Avoid CC'ing everyone. Target the communication

Step 3: Deliver → Choose the Right Channel
Effective communication starts with clear expectations. Your team needs to know when, where, and how to communicate to avoid confusion and inefficiency.
- Urgent? Use chat or video call
- Complex? Use a meeting with visuals
- Routine? Use a shared doc or async update

Step 4: Document → Make It Traceable
Ensure your team has a centralized location for all important information. Store key documents, project updates, and decisions on a shared drive to ensure everyone has access to the same information. If there are documents that multiple people are updating, be sure you have place where everyone is working on the most current document.
- Summarize key points and decisions

- Use shared spaces like project boards, Slack channels, or internal wikis

Quick Wins
Looking for a quick win this week, implement the following:
- Audit your weekly communications. What can you simplify or eliminate?
- Standardize team updates (e.g., Monday kickoff email, Friday recap post)
- Clarify "channel norms" with your team (what goes where and why)

Leadership in Action
After adopting the No Excuses Communication Strategy, my client was able to improve communication between all departments and eliminate the competitive environment that was destroying collaboration. By the end of her first year, she had improved collaboration and established open communication between all departments regardless of where they worked. Her team learned they needed each other to effectively provide customer service to all their clients. Profits and productivity grew quickly as her team communicated more and worked together to accomplish the company's overall goals. Without effective communication, she would have failed, and the company probably would have gone out of business.

Real World Example
Automattic, the company behind WordPress.com, Jetpack, and WooCommerce, has over 2,000 employees spread across 95 countries speaking 120 different languages with no central office. The company is committed to diversity, equity, and inclusion, with the goal to democratize publishing and commerce so that anyone with a story can tell it, and anyone with a product can sell it, regardless of income, gender,

politics, language, or where they live in the world.

What sets Automattic apart is their fully remote workforce, a bold departure from traditional office-based environments. This unique structure thrives on a culture of trust and autonomy, allowing employees the freedom to work in ways that best suit them. Their remote-first model runs on asynchronous communication and intentional documentation. Slack and Zoom are used sparingly. Instead, most conversations happen in writing through internal blogs (called "P2s"), where decisions are visible to everyone. Leaders write to be understood, not just to be heard.

This async-first culture gives people time to think before they speak, reduces meeting fatigue, and creates a searchable archive of institutional knowledge. But it only works because communication is intentional, not reactive. "Communication is oxygen. And like oxygen, you don't notice it until it's gone—or low quality." Matt Mullenweg, CEO of Automattic[12]

I love their focus on output, not on the traditional, superficial markers of what is considered to be a 'good' employee. They don't expect strict working hours, endless meetings, or formal attire. They focus on what's needed to accomplish their goals and they communicate this to their team consistently and intentionally. When given time to process information and complete tasks, you will find that your team is actually more productive and effective at their jobs.

In summary, employees respond to effective communication with trust, engagement, and higher productivity. A leader who communicates well not only empowers their team to excel but also creates a more cohesive and supportive work environment, ultimately driving long-term success.

In the next chapter, we'll explore how to cultivate a strong team culture virtually. It's the key to keeping your remote team motivated and engaged in a way that promotes team cohesion.

Excuse-Proof Reflection

Journal your responses:

1. Are you communicating with intention, or out of habit? Describe how you communicate.

   _____

   _____

   _____

   _____

2. Where are misunderstandings or delays happening on your team?

   _____

   _____

   _____

   _____

3. What's one communication channel you can streamline or use more effectively?

   _____

   _____

   _____

   _____

4. Reflect on how your team communicates today. Are you using meetings as a crutch for unclear messaging?

   _____

   _____

   _____

   _____

5. What's one communication habit you could improve this week for better clarity or connection?

_____

_____

_____

_____

Resource Download
Download the 4D Method Message Planner, Effective Communication Checklist, and Weekly Team Communication Template at TracieLJames.com/remoteleader to create clarity with every message you send to everyone, especially your team.

Chapter 4

Chapter 4

Cultivate Team Cohesion

"Connection is why we're here. It's what gives purpose and meaning to our lives." Brené Brown

Cohesion fuels collaboration. When individuals within a team feel a genuine sense of connection, trust, and mutual respect, they are far more likely to engage fully with one another and with the work. Cohesion creates a supportive environment where people feel psychologically safe to share ideas, ask questions, and challenge assumptions without fear of judgment or exclusion. This kind of relational safety empowers team members to lean into collaboration with authenticity and openness.

When people feel connected to each other, they contribute more fully to the mission. A strong sense of belonging and shared purpose transforms passive participants into active contributors. Rather than just completing tasks, team members are inspired to bring their creativity, insight, and discretionary effort to the table. They align their personal goals with the team's objectives, which amplifies overall engagement and productivity. In essence, connection drives commitment and that commitment drives results.

This chapter explores practical strategies for building meaningful relationships and cultivating a unified team culture, even when physical proximity is not an option.

Leadership Reality Check

I've worked in call centers at different points in my career, both in person and remote. The one thing that was the same regardless of company or location was the disconnection that exists within the call center. There were rarely interactions beyond task and sales updates. Whenever a client escalation required a cross-functional response, it was not handled well, and the client suffered as a result. Often, no one stepped up to address the issue fully and afterward everyone played the blame game. It wasn't a performance issue. It was a cohesion issue. We didn't feel like a team.

Teams don't bond by accident. They bond by design. In remote settings, teams can become highly efficient, but emotionally disconnected. Without casual encounters and shared space, people start to feel like cogs instead of colleagues. And once relationships weaken, collaboration, loyalty, and morale follow.

To build cohesion remotely, you must address the issues head on and not make any excuses for why it can't be done. When you have a team that resides in different geographic locations, you must be flexible when scheduling team events. For example, you can use asynchronous communication tools and rotate virtual events to accommodate all time zones. You can also create structured opportunities for casual interactions, like virtual watercooler channels. To reduce the feelings of disconnection, you could pair new or isolated team members with mentors or buddies to cultivate inclusion.

Principle in Focus

High-performing remote teams are built on more than shared goals. They're built on human connection. The best leaders don't just organize tasks. They design a culture of belonging and connection. They create space

---

for laughter, celebration, and vulnerability, even across screens and time zones.

In remote work environments, where employees are dispersed across cities, countries, and sometimes continents, the sense of connection and a cohesive team culture can easily erode.
One of the most challenging aspects of remote leadership is cultivating a sense of connection and culture without the benefit of physical proximity. Yet, a strong team culture is essential for maintaining engagement, collaboration, and morale. Without intentional effort, team members may feel isolated, disengaged, or disconnected from the broader mission. However, when leaders prioritize connection and culture, they create a foundation that not only boosts morale but also drives collaboration and innovation.

Cultivating cohesion requires you to create a connected culture. Culture isn't just about perks or social events. It's the shared values, behaviors, and practices that define how your team works together. A strong culture provides clarity, cohesion, and motivation. Clarity enables the team to be aligned on goals and expectations. Cohesion strengthens relationships and builds trust. Motivation keeps team members engaged and enthusiastic. Without deliberate effort, culture can erode in a remote setting, leading to disengagement and misalignment.

Team cohesion is the sense of connection, camaraderie, and shared responsibility among members. It doesn't require constant interaction, but it does require intentional design. In dispersed teams, cohesion won't happen by accident. As a leader, you shape the environment where trust, empathy, and collaboration can grow.

Why It Matters

Remote work has many advantages, such as flexibility and access to global talent, but it also presents unique challenges. The lack of casual interactions exists. Without watercooler chats or impromptu lunches, opportunities for informal bonding diminish. The workplace can become fragmented. Different time zones, backgrounds, and work environments can make it harder to maintain a unified identity. An emotional disconnect can develop. Team members can feel "out of sight, out of mind," leading to reduced engagement.

Despite these challenges, cultivating connection and culture in remote teams yields significant benefits. With focused effort, you can create higher engagement. Connected employees are more motivated and invested in their work. Developing stronger collaboration improves trust and teamwork. You can reduce turnover by ensuring employees feel valued and connected. As a leader, you hold the key to overcoming these challenges and reaping these benefits by intentionally cultivating connection and culture.

Cohesive teams:
- Navigate change with more resilience
- Resolve conflict more productively
- Innovate through open collaboration

According to research by Deloitte[13], teams with strong cohesion report 25% higher engagement and 50% greater productivity.

Common Pitfalls

Building culture is not easy, but it can be done. Focus on the solutions you need to overcome these potential pitfalls.
- Transactional culture: Only talking about tasks, never about people

---

- Isolation: Some team members go weeks without meaningful interaction
- Lack of shared rituals: No structure to foster connection and belonging
- Unacknowledged differences: Ignoring diverse working styles, time zones, or cultures

No-Excuses Cohesion Strategy
Team culture is the backbone of how a group functions, communicates, and grows. In remote settings, culture must be actively nurtured. Creating meaningful connections in a virtual environment requires deliberate action. Start the process by following the 3Rs to build a cohesive team culture using the 3Rs:

No Excuses
Cohesion Strategy

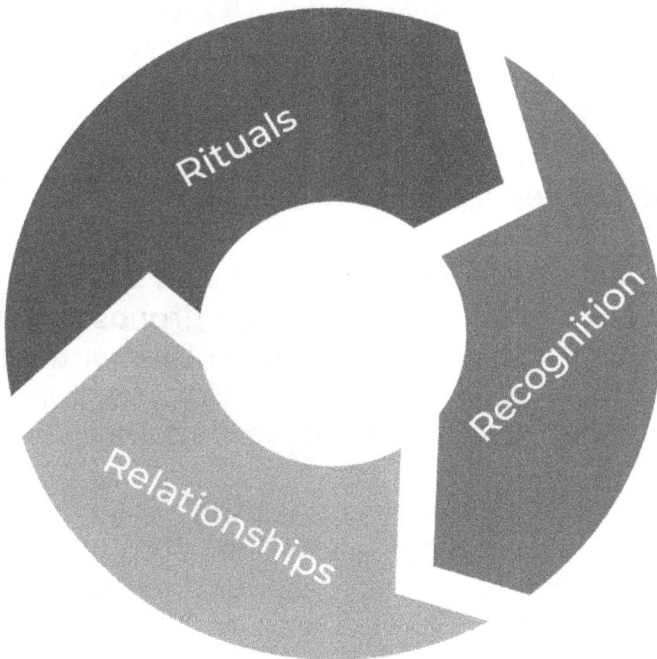

Rituals

Recognition

Relationships

Step 1: Rituals → Create Predictable Moments of Connection

As we learned in Chapter 2, consistency is key to building trust with your team. They need to know what to expect so be consistent in how you build connection within your team. The goal is for them to learn more about each other, feel valued and appreciated by you and the company, and to ultimately work together better.

- Weekly standups with a personal check-in
- Monthly "team wins" shout-outs
- Virtual coffee chats or peer pairings

2. Recognition → Celebrate Progress and People

Create consistent opportunities for recognition by not only celebrating wins, but also celebrating birthdays, work anniversaries, and personal accomplishments. Implement a system where they can show appreciation to each other. Be sure to spread the love throughout your team. Don't be seen as playing favorites with your team members.

- Call out behaviors that align with team values
- Recognize effort, not just outcomes
- Use both public and private channels

3. Relationships → Foster Trust and Empathy

Allow your team to connect in small groups and 1x1 to build a better connection with each other without you involved. It's important that you show your team how much you value their ability to work together in a cohesive manner.

- Encourage 1x1 peer connections
- Model vulnerability and active listening
- Make space for learning about each other beyond roles

Quick Wins
Looking for a quick win this week, implement the following:

- Add a "human check-in" question to your next team meeting (e.g., "What's one win you had outside of work this week?")
- Schedule one virtual team-building activity this month (e.g., trivia, show-and-tell, theme days)
- Recognize someone's contribution in a team-wide channel this week

Leadership in Action
As a call center team lead, I created an opportunity weekly where team members shared a professional and personal highlight. I also launched monthly peer recognition shout-outs and paired teammates for 15-minute "connect calls" to help new employees to connect with veterans. Within two months, my team began collaborating more proactively and cross-supporting during peak periods. I couldn't impact the entire call center, but I was able to build more cohesion within my team. I've remained in touch with many of them since leaving the company.

Real World Example
Doist, the team behind productivity apps like Todoist and Twist, is fully remote, async-first company that operates in over 30 countries. Despite the distance, their leadership has cultivated a sense of closeness that many companies' envy.

Here's how they've been able to do it[14]:

- Every new hire gets a mentor for their first 90 days.
- They host monthly "social calls" where work talk is off-limits.
- Team members write "user manuals" describing their work style, preferences, and quirks.

- Leaders model whole-person engagement, asking about life beyond work.

This intentional focus on relationship-building makes collaboration smoother, feedback more honest, and team morale consistently high. "Culture isn't what you write on the wall. It's what you do when no one's watching." Amir Salihefendić, CEO of Doist

In summary, connection and culture are not optional in remote work, but essential. They form the foundation of trust, collaboration, and resilience, enabling your team to thrive even in the face of challenges while considering their mental and physical health. As a leader, your commitment to cultivating these elements will pay dividends in engagement, retention, and overall success.

In the next chapter, we'll explore how to lead with a focus on outcomes instead of activity to ensure long-term growth and sustainability for your team.

Excuse-Proof Reflection

Journal your responses:

1. How connected does your team feel to one another and to me? Describe an example of connection or disconnection that currently exists.

   _____

   _____

   _____

   _____

2. Does your team have regular rituals that reinforce your team identity? List any rituals you have now.

   _____

   _____

   _____

   _____

3. What's one thing you can do this week to strengthen relationships on the team?

   _____

   _____

   _____

   _____

4. Think of someone on your team who might feel disconnected. When was the last time you reached out to them personally? What small step can you take this week to create more connection without adding another meeting?

   _____

   _____

   _____

   _____

Resource Download
Download the Team Rituals Planning Guide and Peer
Recognition Guide at TracieLJames.com/remoteleader
to make team cohesion a habit, not a hope.

Chapter 5

Chapter 5

Outcomes Not Activity

"What gets measured gets managed." Peter Drucker

Great leaders prioritize impact over busyness because they understand that true progress is measured by meaningful results, not by how busy or overwhelmed their teams appear. They resist the temptation to equate activity with achievement, focusing instead on strategic actions that move the needle toward key objectives. Rather than rewarding constant motion or packed schedules, they champion clarity, intentionality, and outcomes. These leaders ask, "What will make the biggest difference?" and they align time, energy, and resources accordingly. By leading with this mindset, they foster a culture where purpose guides productivity, and where every action contributes to measurable, lasting impact.

Leadership Reality Check

Early in my sales career, I had a manager who loved to micromanage his team. It drove me nuts. He constantly assigned additional work because he felt like he needed to know our every move every day, even though we were primarily in the office with him. He wanted daily emails in the morning outlining the tasks for the day and another at the end of the day with what was completed. In addition, there was a weekly update he wanted every Friday afternoon. He was constantly frustrated with us because he felt we weren't getting enough done each day. We were frustrated that we weren't making the sales and our checks were less than they should've been. No one was winning here.

In remote work environments, many leaders struggle with the lack of visibility into what their team members are doing day-to-day. This uncertainty can lead to micromanagement, i.e., constant check-ins, excessive monitoring, and a focus on how work is being done rather than the value it's delivering. The unintended result? Team members feel distrusted and disengaged, and leaders end up overwhelmed trying to manage every detail.

In remote teams, what you measure signals what you value. When leaders can't "see" their team working, they may start tracking superficial metrics like response time, Slack activity, hours online. But these aren't true indicators of impact. Over-focusing on visibility can breed mistrust and micromanagement. Real productivity can't be tracked by presence alone.

Micromanagement is the silent killer of team morale, innovation, and trust.[15] For remote teams, where visibility is limited, the temptation to micromanage can be overwhelming. But this leadership style often achieves the opposite of its intended effect and stifles productivity and creates a toxic work environment. One of the greatest challenges and opportunities of leading remote teams is shifting from managing tasks to empowering results. In a remote environment, trust and autonomy are critical to cultivating a high-performing team.

Are You a Micromanager?
Micromanagement can be difficult to recognize, especially when it's motivated by a desire to ensure success. However, certain behaviors are telltale signs:
- You provide overly detailed directions for tasks, leaving little room for team members' creativity.
- You constantly ask for updates, interrupting workflows and signaling a lack of trust.

- You hesitate to delegate important responsibilities, fearing they won't be handled correctly.

Take a moment to reflect on your leadership style. Are you frequently correcting your team's work or redoing tasks yourself? Do you feel anxious when a team member handles a critical project? Acknowledging these tendencies is the first step toward change.

Principle in Focus
Traditional leadership often emphasizes visible activity as a measure of productivity. In a remote setting, this approach is not only impractical but also counterproductive. Shift your focus to outcomes. Define clear objectives and measure success based on deliverables and results, not hours logged or online presence. Instead of checking if an employee is online at 9 a.m., set a goal for a project milestone and trust them to manage their time effectively.

Employees will respond positively to an outcome focused approach because it emphasizes trust, autonomy, and accountability. Employees feel empowered when the quality and impact of their work matters more than the number of hours spent working. They are more likely to take ownership of their tasks, striving to deliver meaningful results more efficiently. They will feel less pressure to "look busy". Flexible work schedules enable employees to manage their personal responsibilities, which reduces stress and burnout. Overall, employees appreciate being trusted to manage their time and resources.

In the long term, employees are more likely to experiment, innovate, and find creative solutions. By focusing on shared goals and outcomes, teams often communicate more effectively and align their efforts toward collective success. Today professionals value flexibility and autonomy, making these organizations more attractive to high-performing individuals.

When executed effectively, a focus on outcomes over time worked can transform a team's culture, enhancing both performance and employee satisfaction. An effective leader cultivates an environment of clear expectations, open communication, and consistent accountability to ensure their team succeeds no matter where they work.

Smart remote leaders shift the focus from activity to outcomes. They measure progress, quality, impact and they involve the team in defining those metrics. This creates clarity, ownership, and motivation without surveillance.

Trust is built on outcomes, not oversight. Focusing on output over activity shifts the leader's attention from how work is getting done to what is being achieved. This results-oriented leadership approach empowers team members to use their strengths, encourages accountability, and allows leaders to coach instead of control.

Focusing on outcomes means defining, measuring, and driving results, not just tasks. In remote and hybrid teams, this principle becomes mission critical. Visibility is limited, so clarity on what actually matters must be intentional. Busy doesn't equal effective. You can be fully scheduled and still not move the needle.

Why It Matters
Ironically, micromanagement creates the very issues it seeks to prevent, like missed deadlines, low-quality work, and disengaged employees. When leaders

———

micromanage, team members feel their abilities are doubted. This erodes trust and weakens relationships. It also reduces engagement. A lack of autonomy leads to disinterest and disengagement. Team members lose their motivation to excel when they feel over-controlled. Often micromanagement will increase employee turnover. Working for a micromanager can be very stressful. Most importantly, it stifles innovation and creativity. Creativity thrives on freedom. Micromanagement discourages out-of-the-box thinking and problem-solving.

According to Gallup[16], clarity of expectations is one of the strongest predictors of employee engagement and performance. When leaders shift from activity to outcomes:
- Teams make smarter decisions autonomously
- Performance conversations become clearer and more fair
- Energy is aligned around goals, not guesswork

Common Pitfalls
- Measuring effort over results: Rewarding "working late" rather than delivering value
- Vague goals: "Do your best" becomes the norm
- Micromanaging tasks: Discourages ownership and slows momentum
- No feedback loops: No system to assess progress against desired outcomes

No-Excuses Outcome Alignment Strategy
Use No-Excuses Outcome Alignment Strategy to shift your team's focus to what truly matters:

Outcome Alignment Strategy

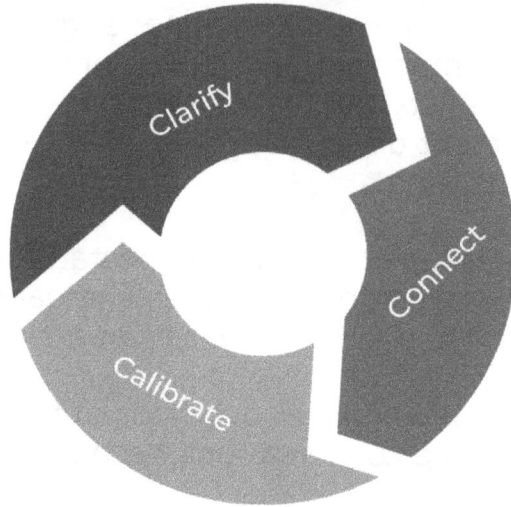

Step 1: Metrics → Clarify What Success Looks Like

Measuring the right metrics and cultivating a culture of continuous improvement ensures your team consistently performs at its best. There can be no excuses when the metrics are clearly defined and tracked consistently.

- Define outcomes, not just deliverables
- Ask: "How will we know if this is working?"

Step 2: Track → Connect Outcomes to Purpose

The metrics you track should connect to the purpose and overall vision for the company and your team. If it's out of alignment, you will achieve something that doesn't move the needle in the right direction.

- Help the team see why it matters
- Use language that ties work to broader goals (team, customer, org)

- Ask: "How does this goal/task connect to our overall goals?"

Step 3: Assess → Calibrate Regularly

Regularly reflect on what worked, what didn't, and how to improve. Utilizing tools and techniques can enhance the accuracy and efficiency of performance measurement. You must decide which tool and/or technique will work best for you and your team.

- Use check-ins and reviews to course-correct
- Focus on learning, not blame
- Ask this weekly: "Are we working on what matters most right now?"

Quick Wins

Looking for a quick win this week, implement the following:

- Review your top 3 team priorities. Can you clearly state the outcome for each?
- Replace "to-do" lists with "results expected" lists for key initiatives
- In your next team meeting, ask: "What does success look like for this project?"
- Take a look at your team's current metrics or KPIs. Are they driving real outcomes or just activity? What's one metric you could update or remove to better align with your team's true value?

Leadership in Action

My sales manager just refused to understand that his micromanaging style was impeding our ability to get the results he wanted from us. We all finally complained that all his additional reports left us with fewer hours to do our jobs. We needed that time to do the research on potential clients before we made our calls. The constant reporting on every little task required at least 30 minutes to an hour to complete each day because it was so detailed. He just ignored our complaints and said we were lazy. I left the company after only 6 months when I found a new position. Several other salespeople left as well. This was not the result he was looking for, but his leadership style pushed us all away from the company. Remember people don't quit bad companies, they quit bad leaders.

Real World Example
Trello, now part of Atlassian, has long embraced distributed work. Their team manages projects using their own Kanban-style platform, but their real superpower is how they define success.

Rather than tracking online presence, Trello uses visible workflows, goals, and retrospectives to drive accountability. Weekly demos, team scorecards, and individual goals are shared across teams. This gives leaders insight into momentum without micromanaging behavior.

Leaders at Trello don't reward face time. They reward focus, follow-through, and forward motion. "It's not about when or where you work. It's about what you get done." Michael Pryor, Trello Co-founder [17]

In summary, you must shift your focus from managing activity to leading with a focus on outcomes. Apply the Outcome Alignment Strategy so you can define success with clarity, align team efforts to what matters most, and create a culture of accountability without micromanagement. When teams understand the why behind their work and how success is measured, motivation and impact increase. Begin building a results-driven culture starting today.

In the next chapter, we'll delve into how to create a remote leadership playbook to help you eliminate the excuses blocking you from remote team leadership success.

Excuse-Proof Reflection

Journal your responses:

1. Where are you rewarding activity instead of outcomes?

_____

_____

_____

_____

2. Do your team members understand what success looks like?

_____

_____

_____

_____

3. How can you better connect daily work to long-term results?

_____

_____

_____

_____

Resource Download

Download the Outcome Clarity Worksheet and Weekly Results Review at TracieLJames.com/remoteleader to help your team stay focused on what truly drives value.

Chapter 6

Chapter 6

Design Your Leadership Playbook

As we conclude this journey into leading anywhere, we're creating a clear, repeatable leadership system brings structure, consistency, and confidence no matter where your team works. A well-defined plan will help you lead with clarity, confidence, and purpose. Please remember that this is a living document that will change over time as you learn more and as your team changes. Don't get stuck in one way of doing things. Continue to use this process to refine your leadership.

Leadership Reality Check
I created my first playbook when I was working as an event and marketing coordinator for a national company. It was a position that required working with multiple locations all over the state of MS. Each location had its own way of operating. Some participated in all the national initiatives and others did not. I quickly realized everyone on my team was working from a different playbook or none at all. Decision-making consistently stalled. Collaboration was non-existent. Meetings were unproductive. Event production was chaotic and ineffective. I needed a system that I could use with the entire team. So, I created a simple playbook that aligned the entire team around clear goals, productive activities, consistent rules and then everything changed for the better.

Principle in Focus
Your Remote Leadership Playbook is your personal operating system for leading your team from anywhere. It provides clarity around how you:
- Clarity & Purpose
- Build Trust

- Communication
- Team Cohesion
- Outcomes

It's not about control. It's about coherence and collaboration.

Why It Matters
According to MIT Sloan research[18], high-performing virtual teams have one thing in common: they document and follow consistent ways of working. A playbook:
- Reduces ambiguity
- Speeds up onboarding
- Enables self-direction and autonomy

Common Pitfalls
This playbook will help you avoid these pitfalls:
- Inconsistent expectations: Each team member gets a different message
- Lost time and energy: Reinventing the wheel with every project
- Leader dependency: Team can't operate without constant guidance
- Cultural drift: Values get lost without structure

Remote Leadership Playbook
Use everything you've learned so far to create your own customized leadership playbook in the next section of this chapter.

Section 1: Clarity & Purpose

Describe your team's vision, purpose and 3–5 guiding values. These should drive decision-making and behavior.

- What is our team's vision?

  _____

  _____

  _____

  _____

- What is our team's purpose?

  _____

  _____

  _____

  _____

- What do we stand for? What are our values?

  Value #1 _____

  Value #2 _____

  Value #3 _____

  Value #4 _____

  Value #5 _____

- How will decisions be made? Outline which decisions require your input and which decisions team members can make on their own.

  _____

  _____

  _____

  _____

- What expectations do you have for each role/position on your team?

  _____

  _____

  _____

  _____

- *Tip:* Include your one-sentence vision, purpose, and 3-5 team values in plain language.
- *Tools:* Leadership Clarity Audit, Outcome Clarity Worksheet, and Leadership One Pager

Section 2: Build Trust
Outline how you will build trust with your team consistently.

- How will you be transparent with your team and share what you know consistently?

  _____

  _____

  _____

  _____

- How will mistakes and other issues be addressed with your team?

  _____

  _____

  _____

  _____

- How will you protect the time you set aside to work with your team individually and collectively?

  _____

  _____

  _____

  _____

- How will you support your team, provide accountability, and still treat everyone with the respect them as human beings?

  _____
  _____
  _____
  _____

- Team schedule for recurring 1x1s with each team member, weekly team meetings, and quarterly planning sessions below:

  _____
  _____
  _____
  _____

- What open ended question(s) do you commit to asking in your team meetings?

  _____
  _____
  _____
  _____

- How will you acknowledge your team publicly for their behaviors that build trust, i.e. ownership, vulnerability, collaboration. Commit to at least 1 person per week.

  _____
  _____
  _____
  _____

- *Tip: Be sure to include strategies for recognition along the journey to a goal, not just the destination.*
- *Tools: Team Trust Survey and 1X1 Conversation Guide*

Section 3: Communication

Determine how your team will communicate, include details on regular meetings, communication tools, availability, and workflows. Clearly set expectations.

- What are our norms around communication, collaboration, and meetings?

  _____

  _____

  _____

  _____

- What tools and channels do we use and for what purpose? Determine communication response times. Set async vs sync expectations.

  _____

  _____

  _____

  _____

- After you complete the audit of your weekly communications, answer this question: what can you simplify or eliminate?

  _____

  _____

  _____

  _____

- How will you standardize team updates?

  _____

  _____

  _____

  _____

- ***Tip:*** *Create a "How We Communicate" section that covers time zones, response times, and meeting schedules.*

- **Tools:** *Effective Communication Checklist, 4D Method Message Planner, and Weekly Team Communication Template*

Section 4: Team Cohesion
Describe how you maintain connection, celebrate wins, and reinforce your culture. Include rituals, peer recognition, and moments of reflection.

- What rituals does your team need to remain connected no matter where they're working each day?

  _____
  _____
  _____
  _____

- What virtual team-building activity will you add to the schedule this month?

  _____
  _____
  _____
  _____

- How will you recognize your team? How will team members recognize each other?

  _____
  _____
  _____
  _____

- How do peers build relationship with each other consistently? How do we stay connected?

  _____
  _____
  _____
  _____

- *Tip: Involve your team in developing rituals to ensure you have buy-in, otherwise it will be a waste of time and effort to implement.*
- *Tools: Team Rituals Planning Guide, Peer Recognition Template and Onboarding/Offboarding Process Guide.*

Section 5: Outcomes

List your top priorities, key outcomes, and how they will be measured. Be detailed for each role on your team.

- What are our top 3-5 priorities? Clearly state the outcome for each below.

  _____
  _____
  _____
  _____

- Assess your team's current metrics/KPIs. Are they driving real outcomes or just activity? What's one metric you could update or remove to better align with your team's true value?

  _____
  _____
  _____
  _____

- How will outcomes be assessed over time? How will you determine if any changes need to be made in what's tracked?

  _____
  _____
  _____
  _____

- Consider a current project "to-do" list. Revise the list with a focus on the "results expected". Outline below.

_____

_____

_____

_____

- *Tip: Use outcome-based language and connect each goal to the overall company goals.*
- *Tools: Weekly Results Template and Performance Metrics Table*

Quick Wins
Create this playbook this week. Don't wait! No Excuses!!
- Block one hour this week to sketch the first two sections of your playbook
- Share a rough draft with your team for feedback and co-creation
- Choose one section to implement immediately

Leadership in Action
After building a marketing events playbook, I was able to reduce the event planning time for each location by 50%, improved communication, and experienced a 10% increase in local event attendance by staff and 15% increase in attendance by potential clients. My team reported feeling more confident, independent, and aligned. They were able to learn from each other's successes and failures to improve the market overall.

In summary, designing your own Leadership Playbook to have a simple, powerful system to lead with clarity, consistency, and confidence from anywhere. This document will help you keep your team aligned on vision, communicate effectively, build trust, and drive results consistently. When you eliminate ambiguity and empower your team to work more independently without you having to hover. This playbook will give you a repeatable framework that scales with your team and evolves with your leadership. Make it your go-to guide for leading anywhere.

Excuse-Proof Reflection

Journal your responses:

1. What unspoken expectations need to be documented?

   _____

   _____

   _____

   _____

2. What parts of my leadership are reactive instead of intentional and repeatable?

   _____

   _____

   _____

   _____

3. If I stepped away for a week, what would my team need to know to stay on track?

   _____

   _____

   _____

   _____

Resource Download

Download your Remote Leadership Playbook Template at TracieLJames.com/remoteleader and start customizing your system for clarity, consistency, and confidence.

Conclusion

Conclusion

Leading from Anywhere, Excuse Free

You've made it to the final chapter, but in many ways, this is just the beginning. This is a new phase in your personal leadership journey.

You now have the tools to lead with clarity, build trust, communicate intentionally, cultivate cohesion, focus on outcomes, and design your own leadership system. These aren't just good ideas, but they're the new essentials.

In a world where everything moves fast and teams are rarely in the same place at the same time, your ability to lead with purpose and structure is what will set you apart. The best leaders don't wait for perfect conditions. They create alignment in ambiguity, build culture across distance, and move people toward meaningful results wherever they are.

Let's be honest: leadership is never easy. But it also isn't mysterious. It's a series of intentional choices, repeatable habits, and courageous conversations. It's the discipline of clarity over confusion, action over avoidance, and outcomes over excuses.

So, here's your challenge: Don't wait for permission. Don't wait for ideal conditions. And don't wait for someone else to fix what's broken. Step forward. Take what you've learned. Put it into motion.

Leading anywhere isn't about achieving perfection. It's about striving for excellence while adapting to the realities of remote work. By applying the principles and strategies outlined in this book, you'll create a team that thrives in any environment. You don't have to be in the same room to be an extraordinary leader.

Remember, great leadership starts with intention and grows through action. Your remote leadership playbook is your compass; use it to navigate challenges, celebrate victories, and unlock the full potential of your team. You just have to lead on purpose, in purpose and with purpose.

This is your call to action.
This is your playbook.
This is your time.
Thank you for embarking on this journey. Now, go forth and lead your remote team from anywhere. No excuses.

The Excuse Proof Leadership Manifesto:

- I lead with purpose, not just position.
- I build systems, not silos.
- I choose clarity over comfort.
- I create trust by how I show up.
- I align my team around what matters most.
- I lead from anywhere, but I lead with intent.

Remote Leadership Playbook Template

All resources in this section are available to download here: TracieLJames.com/remoteleader

Remote Leadership Playbook Creation

Purpose: This playbook helps you lead high-performing teams from anywhere. Each section includes space to document and share the systems that make your team run effectively. Compile everything you've created so far into one document that will guide your team leadership to promote consistency.

Section 1: Team Vision & Values

Our Team's Vision

_____

_____

_____

_____

Our Team's Values

_____

_____

_____

_____

Section 2: How We Work

Communication Norms *(Be sure to note time zones.)*

_____

_____

_____

_____

Collaboration Norms *(Be sure to note time zones.)*

_____

_____

_____

_____

Regular Meeting Schedule *(Be sure to note time zones.)*

_____

_____

_____

_____

List the tools/channels we use and for what purpose.
(Be sure to note response times.)

_____

_____

_____

_____

Section 3: Goals & Metrics

What are our core team priorities?

_____

_____

_____

_____

How do we measure success?

_____

_____

_____

_____

Section 4: Decision-Making & Autonomy

What decisions require leader input?

_____

_____

_____

_____

What decisions can team members own?

_____

_____

_____

_____

Section 5: Culture & Recognition

How do we stay connected? Include team rituals and
check-ins.

_____

_____

_____

_____

How do we celebrate and support each other?

_____

_____

_____

_____

Section 6: Onboarding Process (optional)

How do we onboard new hires?

_____

_____

_____

_____

How do we ensure new hires feel connected?

_____

_____

_____

_____

90 Day
Leadership Guide

All resources in this section are available to download here: TracieLJames.com/remoteleader

90-Day Leadership Tracker (Sample)

Purpose: Help you stay focused and accountable throughout your leadership journey.

Create your own tracker in Excel or GoogleSheets

Columns:
- Week Number
- Key Focus (from the book)
- Top 1–2 Actions
- Completed? (Yes/No)
- Key Insight or Learning
- Notes

Sample Entry:

Week	Focus	Top Action	Done?	Insight	Notes
1	Clarit	Draft and share team vision statement	Yes	Helped align everyone's weekly goals	Update 1-pager next week
2	Trust	1x1 Trust Check-In with each member	No	People want more visibility on strategy	Schedule for next week
3	Communicate	Audit weekly communication	No	Is it effective?	Get team feedback
4	Cohesion	Add human check-in to next meeting	Yes	Team is responding	Add to meeting agenda
5	Outcomes	Clarify the 3 top team priorities	NO	Ensure team knows where to focus	Ask for clarity and track results

This guide is a living document to grow and evolve your leadership practice. Update regularly and revisit after every 90-day cycle.

Leadership Clarity Audit

Purpose: Assess how clearly your team understands goals, roles, and expectations.

Instructions: Use this in a team meeting, one-on-one, or anonymous survey format.

Clarity Audit Questions

Rate each statement from 1 (Strongly Disagree) to 5 (Strongly Agree)

1. I understand the overall vision and mission of our team.
2. I know how my work contributes to our team's goals.
3. I have clarity on what success looks like in my role.
4. I know who is responsible for what within the team.
5. Our goals and priorities are clearly communicated.
6. I receive regular feedback that helps me stay aligned.
7. I know what decisions I can make independently.

Team Discussion Prompts

1. Where are we aligned?
2. Where are the biggest gaps in clarity?
3. What can we improve immediately?

Leadership One-Pager

Purpose: Share your leadership style, expectations, and preferences with your team. Create your one pager to be more consistent in how you lead your team.

Template Structure:

Section 1: My Leadership Philosophy
- What I believe about leadership
- How I define success as a team leader

Section 2: My Communication Style
- Preferred tools (Slack, email, etc.)
- Response time expectations
- Best way to reach me

Section 3: My Expectations
- How we show up as a team
- How I define accountability
- How decisions are made

Section 4: Support & Development
- How I give feedback
- How I support growth
- How I handle conflict

Section 5: Personal Facts *(Optional)*
- Working hours
- Hobbies or fun facts

1x1 Conversation Guide

Use this guide to lead intentional conversations that deepen trust, strengthen relationships, and build psychological safety with each team member.

When to Use:
- During regular 1x1s
- After a conflict or misalignment
- At project kickoffs or transitions
- With new team members

Part 1: Lay the Foundation
- How are you really doing? (Open with empathy. Invite honesty.)
- What's been going well for you lately?
- What's been weighing on you?
- What's one thing I could do to support you better? (Signal that feedback is welcomed and safe.)
- What's something you need from this team to do your best work? (Shift the focus from individual to collective trust.)

TIP: Be sure to listen for understanding and respond accordingly. Be aware of your tone, body language and facial expressions. Remain open even when hearing criticism.

Part 2: Feedback & Alignment
- How clear do you feel on what's expected of you right now? (Use this to clarify roles, goals, and support needs.)

- Is there anything I've done (or haven't done) that impacted your trust in me? (Pause. Listen without defensiveness.)

- What's something you appreciate about the way we work together? (Affirm positive dynamics and reinforce trust.)

TIP: Be sure to ask questions to ensure you're on the same page. Be willing to adjust if needed to ensure trust is being built with everyone on your team.

Part 3: Looking Ahead
- What does a great week look like for you? (Explore motivation and alignment.)
- Where do you want to grow next and how can I help? (Build trust by investing in development.)

TIP: Be open minded about their suggestions and take notes to ensure you remember what motivates and inspires each of your team members.

Team Trust Survey

Use this brief, anonymous survey to assess the current level of trust on your team. Responses will help you spot strengths and surface issues early.

Instructions:
Distribute as a monthly or quarterly check-in via Google Forms, Microsoft Forms, or any survey tool that keeps the results anonymous.

Survey Questions
(Rate each from 1 = Strongly Disagree to 5 = Strongly Agree)

- I feel safe sharing honest feedback with my team.
- My manager follows through on what they say they'll do.
- I believe my teammates have good intentions.
- I can take risks on this team without fear of blame.
- My contributions are recognized and valued.
- Conflicts on this team are handled respectfully and fairly.
- I understand how decisions are made on our team.
- I trust that if I need support, someone will help me.

Open-Ended Questions
- What builds trust on this team?
- What erodes trust on this team?
- One thing I wish we'd do differently to improve team trust is...

4D Method Message Planner

Purpose: Use the 4D Method Message Planner to prepare intentional communication, especially for updates, changes, or team-wide decisions. It ensures clarity, context, and consistency in your messaging.

The 4D Communication Method

- Define – What's the message?
- Decide – Who needs to know?
- Deliver – What's the right channel?
- Document – Where can people find important information?

1. **DEFINE** – What's the message? What should the team know? What do you need the team to do? What's the timeframe? Summarize all the details clearly and concisely.

2. **DECIDE** –Who needs to know? Clearly identify who needs to receive this message. Don't CC everyone. Be intentional.

3. **DELIVER** – What's the right channel? Every message shouldn't be an email. Be intentional as you decide where you will deliver different messages to your team. Allow space for questions and feedback.

4. **DOCUMENT** – Where can they find important information? Where will you store key documentation consistently?

Effective Communication Checklist

Purpose: Use this checklist before sending an important message or scheduling a meeting.

The 5Ps of Effective Communication

Purpose
- Why are we communicating?
- What's the desired outcome?

Platform
- Is this the right medium (Slack, Zoom, email, etc.)?

People
- Who needs to be included?
- Who doesn't?

Pace
- Is this urgent or can it wait?
- Is the timing right?

Posture
- Am I being clear, respectful, and aligned with our values?

Checklist
1. Clear objective?   Yes/No
2. Right audience?   Yes/No
3. Right channel?   Yes/No
4. Respectful tone?   Yes/No
5. Necessary now?   Yes/No

Weekly Team Communication Template

Use this template to create a predictable, transparent weekly update. It can be sent via email, Slack, or your team platform every Monday or Friday.

Weekly Communication Structure

1. Priorities This Week: What's most important for the team to focus on this week? List 3–5 items.

2. Key Updates: What decisions, changes, or information does the team need to know?

3. Wins & Highlights: Recognize achievements, milestones, or team shout-outs.

4. Roadblocks/Risks: Where might we need support, clarity, or quick decision-making?

5. Team Pulse Check: Ask a one-question check-in like "How's your energy this week?" or "What's your top focus today?"

Team Rituals Planning Guide

Purpose: Use this guide to design meaningful, repeatable team rituals that build connection, culture, and cohesion no matter where your team is located. Be sure to include your team in this process.

Step 1: Define the Purpose

Why are you creating this ritual? What aspect of team culture does it reinforce?

Examples: celebrate wins, share learning, build belonging, reduce burnout

Step 2: Choose the Format

How will the ritual be delivered?
- Live: Zoom/Teams meeting
- Async: Slack/Email/Notion
- Hybrid: Combines live and async participation

Step 3: Design the Experience

Answer the following:
- When will it happen? (e.g., weekly, monthly, quarterly)
- Who participates? (e.g., whole team, cross-functional group)
- What happens during the ritual?
- How long will it take? (Aim for 15–30 minutes max)

Step 4: Make It Stick

How will you reinforce participation and make it feel meaningful?

Tips: assign a rotating host, tie it to values, include visuals or music, keep it fun and consistent.

Sample Rituals

- Monday Momentum – Each teammate shares their top focus for the week.
- Wednesday Wins – Share something you're proud of or grateful for.
- Friday Cheers – End the week with peer shout-outs and celebrations.
- New Hire Spotlight – 5 fun questions answered by each new team member in Slack.

Peer Recognition Guide

Purpose: Use these templates to encourage peer-to-peer appreciation and build a culture of recognition.

Slack/Email Shout-Outs

Template 1: The Specific Shout-Out"Big thanks to [Name] for [specific action]. It made a real difference by [impact]."

Example: Big thanks to Jordan for stepping in on the client call last minute. You kept things calm and professional, and the client left impressed.

Template 2: The Values Aligned Shout-Out"[Name] really lived our value of [team/company value] when they [action or behavior]."

Example: Priya really lived our value of collaboration when she helped me troubleshoot a launch issue late Friday.

Monthly Recognition Roundup (Async Form or Meeting Segment)

- Who went above and beyond this month?
- Who demonstrated one of our core values?
- Who deserves a quiet thank-you?

Outcome Clarity Worksheet

Purpose: Use this worksheet to define, align, and communicate the outcomes that matter most. It's especially helpful when setting goals, kicking off projects, or shifting from busywork to results.

Step 1: Define the Desired Outcome
- What is the result we want to achieve?

Example: Launch new onboarding flow with a 90% completion rate within 30 days.

Step 2: Align to Purpose or Value
- Why does this outcome matter?

Example: A smoother onboarding experience improves retention and team ramp-up speed.

Step 3: Clarify Success Metrics
- How will we measure success?

Metrics could include: completion %, error rate, satisfaction score, time to complete, revenue impact, etc.

Step 4: Identify Constraints or Risks
- What could get in the way?

Examples: conflicting priorities, unclear ownership, limited resources.

Step 5: Assign Ownership and Checkpoints
- Who's responsible?
- When will we review progress?

Owner: Sam | Check-in: Weekly stand-up | Final review: June 30

Weekly Results Review Template

Purpose: Use this template to shift team conversations from activity tracking to outcome reflection. Share it in a team doc, Slack, or weekly meeting.

Weekly Results Review

1. Top 3 Outcomes Achieved This Week

- [Result 1 — include metric or impact if possible]

- [Result 2]

- [Result 3]

2. Progress on Key Priorities:

- [Update on project or KPI]

- What Worked Well:
    - [Brief insights, process wins, or teamwork examples]

- What Needs Adjustment:
    - [Bottlenecks, missed targets, unexpected blockers]

3. Next Week's Top 3 Outcomes:

- Planned result #1 [not just tasks]
- Planned result #2 [not just tasks]
- Planned result #3 [not just tasks]

Additional Resources

All resources in this section are available to download here: TracieLJames.com/remoteleader

TECHNOLOGY RESOURCES

Selecting the Right Tools
Choosing the right tools depends on your team's unique needs and workflows. Consider the ease of use, integration capabilities, and scalability before making your selection. Once you've chosen your tools, ensure a smooth rollout by providing training and onboarding, set usage guidelines and monitor consistently and adjust as needed.

Action Step: Evaluate your current tech tools. Identify one tool that could be improved or replaced and take steps to implement a better solution this month.

Remote teams need a comprehensive group of tech tools to address three primary areas: communication, collaboration, and productivity. Below are the must-have tools for each category:

Communication Tools
- Video Conferencing: Zoom or Microsoft Teams
- Instant Messaging: Slack or Microsoft Teams
- Email: Google or Outlook

Collaboration Tools
- Project Management: Asana, Trello, or Monday.com
- Document Sharing: Google Workspace or Microsoft 365
- Whiteboarding: Miro or MURAL

Productivity Tools
- Time Management: Toggl or Clockify
- Automation: Zapier or Power Automate
- Focus Enhancers: Freedom or Focus@Will

COMMUNICATION RESOURCES

Mastering Asynchronous Collaboration

Asynchronous communication, working on your own time instead of in real-time, is the cornerstone of successful remote teams. It's particularly beneficial for teams spread across different time zones. Since many people struggle with this type of collaboration, it's imperative that you help your team make the adjustment.

Encourage each team member to provide detailed updates. In asynchronous environments, clarity is critical. Encourage team members to provide context, updates, and next steps in their messages. Assumptions cannot be made in this format. To ensure everyone receives the detail needed, you can provide a template for status updates. Work with your team to develop this.

Ensure your team has a centralized location for all important information. Store key documents, project updates, and decisions on a shared drive to ensure everyone has access to the same information. If there are documents that multiple people are updating, be sure you have place where everyone is working on the most current document.

Everyone must respect the time boundaries. Avoid expecting instant responses in asynchronous communication. Promote a culture where team members can focus on deep work without constant interruptions. Encourage your team to use "Do Not Disturb" statuses during their focused work hours.

These strategies are imperative to effectively work in an asynchronous environment. At the foundation is respect and trust.

Managing Across Time Zones and Cultures

In an increasingly globalized workplace, remote teams often span multiple time zones and encompass diverse cultural backgrounds. While this diversity brings incredible opportunities for innovation and creativity, it also introduces unique challenges for scheduling, communication, and collaboration. As a leader, mastering the art of managing across time zones and cultures is essential to building a cohesive and effective team.

Coordinating a team spread across continents requires thoughtful planning and flexibility.

- You should leverage time zone overlaps. Identify windows of time where team members' working hours overlap, and schedule critical meetings during these periods.
- To ensure fairness, rotate meeting times so no single region consistently bears the burden of early mornings or late nights.
- Reserve synchronous meetings for high-priority discussions and rely on asynchronous tools for routine updates.
- Define response time expectations for emails and messages to avoid confusion and frustration.
- Cultural diversity can enrich your team but also lead to misunderstandings if not navigated thoughtfully. Here's how to cultivate a culture of respect and inclusion:
- Learn about the cultural norms and communication styles of your team members.
- Create a safe space for team members to share their cultural perspectives and preferences.
- Be flexible in your approach to accommodate different cultural expectations.

- Recognize and honor cultural traditions and holidays.

REMOTE TEAM STRATEGIES

Onboarding & Integrating New Team Members

Effective onboarding is critical to ensuring new team members feel welcomed, supported, and aligned with your team's goals. A well-executed onboarding process can accelerate integration and cultivate immediate engagement.

Begin by creating a comprehensive onboarding plan that covers all the essential information, tools, and team introductions. Work closely with HR and IT to ensure your new hire has access to all the necessary tools. Be sure they receive a team directory, organizational chart, and an overview of their role and responsibilities.

Consider assigning an onboarding buddy for new hires. Pair them with experienced team members who can assist with guiding them through their first few weeks. Their buddy will meet with them regularly their first few weeks to address questions and build rapport.

Schedule time during the first few days to conduct virtual walkthroughs of your tools, platforms, and workflows to ensure new hires can navigate their work environment effectively. Be sure to discuss the communication plan and ensure they understand how each tool is used.

Introduce new team members to the broader team through informal virtual meet-and-greet sessions. You can do this with the entire team and enable them to meet one-on-one. This is the opportunity for them to break the ice.

References

1. Owl Labs Survey - Statistics On Remote Workers That Will Surprise You, January 22, 2025
https://www.apollotechnical.com/statistics-on-remote-workers/

2. Bureau of Labor Statistics
https://www.bls.gov/opub/btn/volume-13/remote-work-productivity.htm

3. Gallup Poll Results
https://business.talkspace.com/articles/impact-of-employee-engagement-on-productivity?utm_

4. Study demonstrates that writing goals enhances goal achievement — Dominican University of California. Matthews, Gail. May 2015, Ninth Annual International Conference of the Psychology Research Unit of Athens Institute for Education and Research (ATINER).

5. Experimental Tests of the Endowment Effect and the Coase Theorem. Daniel Kahneman, Jack L. Knetsch and Richard H. Thaler. Journal of Political Economy, Vol. 98, No. 6 (Dec., 1990), pp. 1325-1348

6. GitLab Public Handbook
https://handbook.gitlab.com/

7. GitLab Handbook Benefits
https://handbook.gitlab.com/handbook/about/

8. Google Project Aristotle
https://rework.withgoogle.com/en/guides/understanding-team-effectiveness

9. Buffer Transparency Dashboard & company blog
   https://buffer.com/open

10.   McKinsey Report
    https://www.abcmoney.co.uk/2025/06/strengthes
    tre-remote-teams-through-smart-internal-
    communication-strategies/

11. The New Science of Building Great Teams.
    Pentland, Alex. Harvard Business Review. April
    2012.

12. Interviews with Matt Mullenweg; Automattic's P2
    communication system

13. Deloitte Research
    https://zight.com/blog/collaboration-statistics/

14. Doist blog and team practices
    https://www.hrcloud.com/blog/remote-
    onboarding-step-by-step-guide

15. Why Aren't You Delegating? Gallo, Amy. Harvard
    Business Review. July 26, 2012

16. Gallop Poll
    https://www.gallup.com/workplace/653711/great
    -detachment-why-employees-feel-stuck.aspx

17. Trello productivity blog, remote team practices
    https://www.atlassian.com/work-
    management/team-management-and-leadership

18. https://executive.mit.edu/managing-virtual-
    teams-for-peak-performance-
    MCR3WAFTZR2RDGJJEP4LC345WWKU.html

ABOUT THE AUTHOR

Tracie L. James
Leadership Strategist, Event Curator, Speaker, & Author

Tracie L James is a remarkable woman who made the shift from being a successful sales and marketing professional to leadership strategist, event curator, speaker, and author. A Mississippi native, Tracie was a go-getter from a young age, always striving for excellence and determined to make her mark in the world.

For over 30 years, Tracie has utilized her expertise in sales and marketing, including retail, account management, customer service, leadership development, marketing, workshop facilitation and training to help corporations, nonprofits, and educational programs.

Based on her event curation and business experience, Tracie has written several books on team building, overcoming excuses, and success in life and business. As a speaker and trainer, she loves helping women build confidence to reach their potential personally and professionally.

With numerous awards and accolades throughout her sales, marketing, speaking, and consulting careers, Tracie is not easily placed in one category, she defines her own.

NOW BOOKING
NOW BOOKING

NOW BOOKING

Ready to Lead Anywhere?!

Tracie James' straight forward yet fun style teaches leaders how to improve their problem solving skills so they will move their team toward more consistent success.

HOW TO BOOK TRACIE

- Keynote
- Team Training
- Executive Coach
- Consulting

tracie L. James

Tracie has been featured on NBC, ABC, and CBS, as well as in newspapers and magazines. Tracie's entertaining style is full of wisdom that will help your leaders achieve better results consistently.

When she presents, Tracie delivers her message with Southern charm infused with wisdom from her 20 years of business experience. She connects with the audience and delivers the "IT" factor that the audience will remember.

> "Very informative message, (Tracie) gave great innovative ideas."
> Mary F.

DATES ARE LIMITED.
REQUEST TRACIE FOR YOUR NEXT EVENT TODAY!
TracieLJames.com